VOLUME ONE

BONFIRE

THE HUNGER FOR MORE

HUNTER MORRIS

To my beautiful family,

Thank you for your never-ending love.

CONTENTS

GIVE YOUR WHOLE LIFE TO JESUS.................................. 5

FOREWORD: DR. JOSHUA FOWLER................................. 6

INTRODUCTION.. 8

CHAPTER ONE: REVEALING THE SIMPLICITY OF JESUS..12

CHAPTER TWO: BREAKING THE MOLD........................... 25

CHAPTER THREE: CAPTURING THE HEART.................... 35

CHAPTER FOUR: REDEFINING & DISCOVERING YOU.... 44

CHAPTER FIVE: CATCH THE FIRE................................. 58

CHAPTER SIX: THERE IS MORE.................................... 73

CHAPTER SEVEN: HUNGER FOR MORE......................... 83

CHAPTER EIGHT: YOU ARE READY............................... 90

ABOUT THE AUTHOR.. 99

GIVE YOUR WHOLE LIFE TO JESUS

I want to ask you personally, have you given your whole life to Jesus? I'm not asking if you've said a prayer before or read the Bible or gone to church. I mean, have you truly given your WHOLE life to Jesus? Does Jesus have every area of your life?

If your answer is no, to any of these, I'd like you to pray this with me:

"Lord Jesus, I thank you for loving me and dying on the cross for me. Jesus, I repent of all my sin. I give my WHOLE life to you right now. I'm not holding anything back! Jesus Christ, I confess that you are the Lord and I believe in my heart that you rose from the grave. I receive you, Jesus. I receive your Holy Spirit. Holy Spirit, consume me. Consume my life, let me never be the same! Thank you Heavenly Father for your love for me and for giving me a new life through your Spirit. I love you Jesus!"

Welcome to the family! Get ready for an amazing journey with Jesus! If you just prayed this prayer, we'd like to hear from you! Please email us let us know that you've given your whole life to Jesus at:
huntermorrisministries@gmail.com

FOREWORD

Are you ready to enter "The More" of the Lord? Are you ready to burn with greater passion for Jesus? If so, the book you're holding is the book for you! I highly recommend both the book and the author! Bonfire is not a theory, it was birthed out of a lifestyle of F.I.R.E. = Faith • Intimacy • Real • Evangelism!

Hunter Morris is a man of fire or should I say, he's a man on fire! He could be called a fireman, but he doesn't put out fires, he starts them. He's a revival fire-starter and an awakening arsonist!

Everywhere Hunter goes, you can experience the Fiery Heat of God's F.I.R.E! When you're around Hunter you will feel the love of the Father and the fiery mantle that rest on him. Whether doing missions work in other nations or just at a local store, Hunter can be found leading people to Jesus and healing the sick.

Bonfire has great depth and is yet understandable for readers of all levels of faith. As you read this book, you will find yourself burning with the presence of the Lord and accessing deeper realms in Jesus.

Bonfire will launch you into the next dimension of your faith and help equip you to burn for Jesus. Expect a tangible difference in your walk with the Lord after reading and applying the principles found in this book.

Hunter, Our Heavenly Father is Papa Proud of you and this anointed book, I know I am!

Read it and Burn!

Dr. Joshua Fowler

Author, Daily Decrees

CEO LegacyLife and #AwakeTheWorld

JoshuaFowler.com

INTRODUCTION

My heart was pounding, my eyes gazing; I knew there had to be more. As I walked among the people, all I could see were lifeless beings. I saw those who didn't believe and I saw those who claimed to be Christians and distinguished no difference. "There has to be more than this," I thought. I believed in a risen Lord yet I didn't see Him alive in anyone around me.

What I believe must have a greater value. If there is no essential value to what I believe, then why must I believe? I saw smiling faces but agonizing pain on the inside. My heart began to groan and cry out to the Lord, "Lord Jesus, I don't want to live like this! I don't want to be like your other children who go back and forth between you and the world. No! I want to burn for you Jesus! This is not enough! Lord, I need you to set me on fire! I want a fire that the world has never seen before. Lord, don't just give me a fire, but give me a bonfire!"

Instantly, something like fire rushed all through my body.

"He will baptize you with the Holy Spirit and fire."
MATTHEW 3:11 ESV

I began to realize that it was Jesus and He had given me what I longed for; to be consumed by His presence. The desire to burn for Jesus was never about seeing myself passionately on fire, but about seeing the whole world burn with the knowledge of Jesus Christ. I asked for more and what happened changed my life forever. Finally, my life had truly begun.

If you're reading this, you may find yourself in a similar place; wondering if there's more, questioning your part or even feeling dead on the inside. Let me be the first to tell you, there's more. Jesus has so much more for your life than where you're at right now. My prayer is that at the end of this book, you will not be the same; that you will look more like Jesus. My desire is that you would have an expectation for this book to help lead you into an encounter with Jesus and help you live a lifestyle that is on fire for God.

More About The Book

This book is designed much like one would build a bonfire. The vision is to build from the ground up. As we build, we'll go deeper and we'll burn for Jesus with a fresh fire.

What is the fire? The fire is that which has been with us since the beginning of time; the Lord. He was there with Moses, guiding the people out of Egypt by a pillar of fire. (EXODUS 13:21-22) He came down in the midst of the people on Mount Sinai, in glory, as fire. (EXODUS 19:18 & EXODUS 24:17) Ezekiel saw a vision of the Lord whose appearance was that of fire. (EZEKIEL 1:26-28) The Holy Spirit came on the believers in Acts with that of tongues or pillars of fire. (ACTS 2:1-4) John saw a vision of the Lord with fire in His eyes. (REVELATION 1:14-18) And the Lord Jesus Christ is coming back in blazing fire. (1 THESSALONIANS 1:5-10) The fire is not a what, the fire is a who. Jesus is the fire; where Jesus is, you can find both His presence

9

and glory. The glory which establishes the nature or realm of God. The presence which is the essence of God. We need Jesus to both establish His nature in us and allow His presence to abide within us so that His image is manifested through us to the world.

"And suddenly there came from heaven a sound like a mighty rushing wind, and it filled the entire house where they were sitting. And divided tongues as of fire appeared to them and rested on each one of them. And they were all filled with the Holy Spirit and began to speak in other tongues as the Spirit gave them utterance."

ACTS 2:2-4 ESV

The baptism in the Holy Spirit and fire empowers us to manifest the image of Christ. The fire is more than an element, but it's a person; the person of Jesus Christ. The fire comes to establish, within us, an atmosphere of glory; the nature in which God always resides. There is no place in Heaven where there is no glory. Jesus moves Heaven and Heaven comes to live within us, not to just rest above us. The Holy Spirit comes to possess us while empowering us to manifest the image of Christ.

There may be things discussed within this book that you are already aware of but I ask that you read this book with fresh eyes. Some things are simplified because of the need for simplicity but all these things have been written so that you will encounter more of Jesus. As you encounter more of Jesus, I pray that the Lord builds a bonfire inside of you and that you set the nations on fire with the knowledge of Jesus Christ. Let all the world know that Jesus is alive and He is coming back soon!

"I have come to set the earth on fire. And how I long for every heart to be already ablaze with this fiery passion for God!"

LUKE 12:49 TPT

CHAPTER ONE
Revealing The Simplicity Of Jesus

What if knowing the person Jesus is more simple than we realize? The Word can often be misunderstood when His image is inaccurately portrayed. The only way to portray Jesus' image accurately is when both the Word of God and the Spirit of God are in tandem. Both the Word of God and the Spirit of God will reveal the person Jesus. If all of Scripture were to be summed up and described as one person, the Word would describe Jesus Christ. Even within the fruits of the Spirit, the person of Jesus Christ is revealed.

"But the fruit of the Spirit [the result of His presence within us] is love [unselfish concern for others], joy, [inner] peace, patience [not the ability to wait, but how we act while waiting], kindness, goodness, faithfulness, gentleness, self-control."

GALATIANS 5:22-23 AMP

In spite of this wonderful revelation, Christianity as a whole, has been overcomplicated. Too often, the focus has been placed on the steps required to get to Jesus rather than just demonstrating and revealing who Jesus is. In a time where everyone is on a smart device, complicated just won't do as everything is easily obtained and quickly accessible. If we, as believers, don't make Jesus obtainable and accessible it will hinder the lost from entering into the fullness of His love. It's impossible to build a relationship with someone you have no interaction with. This is not a call to dumb down the Gospel but rather for us to reveal the simplicity of Jesus. It's a relationship with Jesus. Jesus is received with simplicity yet carries great depth. This is a call to return to simplicity.

Returning To Simplicity

"Truly, I say to you, whoever does not receive the kingdom of God like a child shall not enter it."

MARK 10:15 ESV

Often, we forget that in the middle of Jesus's ministry, women and children surrounded him. During this time, many of the people were uneducated and pushed to the side. Jesus spoke in such a way that only some would understand him. *"For everyone who listens with an open heart will receive progressively more revelation until he has more than enough. But those who don't listen with an open, teachable heart, even the understanding that they think they have will be taken from them."* (MATTHEW 13:12 TPT) However, Jesus lived in a way where all were welcomed by him. *"But Jesus called them to him, saying, "Let the children come to me, and do not hinder them, for to such belongs the kingdom of God."* (LUKE 18:16 ESV)

Jesus motivated people into hunger and out of compassion and love, He himself, was motivated by the people's hunger. Jesus is moved by His love for people;

13

His love for you and I. That's why Jesus died on the cross for us, one word: love. (LUKE 23:26-49)

We want a relationship with Jesus but there is no relationship when there is no love. The love of Jesus invites us to walk in a greater hunger and generous love. If we want to have any kind of relationship with Jesus, we must love and be motivated by pure love.

"We have come into an intimate experience with God's love, and we trust in the love he has for us. God is love! Those who are living in love are living in God, and God lives through them."

1 JOHN 4:16 TPT

Agape love is defined as a divine love; "that which God prefers." Selfless love; needing nothing in return. In the mindset of the world, "you scratch my back and I'll scratch yours," we have been burned by a false image of Jesus. Jesus never considered what He could gain but chose to give love. Let that sink in. He never wanted some form of payment, rather, Jesus chose to become the payment for our sin. That is unconditional love. Unconditional love is a love that sacrifices itself for another, without ever forcing, demanding, or expecting love in return. When we encounter the love of Jesus, we will never be the same. One of the most beautiful things about love, is that love is not an emotion, it is a commitment. Emotions are continually fluctuating and changing, but commitment says, "I will trust you and continue to love you, come what may."

"For the Lord is good; his steadfast love endures forever, and his faithfulness to all generations."

PSALM 100:5 ESV

Our emotions can fluctuate from happiness to sadness within a moments notice; sometimes quicker than others. If our love is only carried through the conduit of our emotions, the end result won't be pure. But if our love is carried through the conduit of our spirit and through commitment, the outcome will be an overflow of love.

"But Christ proved God's passionate love for us by dying in our place while we were still lost and ungodly!"

ROMANS 5:8 TPT

There are many levels and depths of love. At the beginning of a relationship, a couple may say, "I love you," to each other, but their love has not yet been developed or matured. It is a love that doesn't yet carry great depth because there is less revelation of each other. However, when a couple goes through great difficulty and stays together, their love produces the greater depths of love because their commitment has triumphed over their emotion. Love doesn't discount emotion, love just doesn't rest on emotion. The love of Jesus, for us, goes beyond emotion because of His commitment to die on a cross so that we may be saved through Him. Our salvation through Jesus releases His Kingdom within us.

The Simplicity Of The Kingdom Of God

"For the kingdom of God is not a matter of eating and drinking but of righteousness and peace and joy in the Holy Spirit."

ROMANS 14:17 ESV

Righteousness

Righteousness is that which is in right standing with God. We can't get there on our own because we were born into sin. This is where Jesus comes in. Jesus bore all of our sin and shame on the cross. Jesus took the keys to death, hell and the grave and defeated sin once and for all. Jesus loves us more than we could ever imagine, He died so that we could live and live in righteousness; right standing with God. Righteousness is crucial because it is the access point into our relationship with the Father. The only way to God the Father is through Jesus, the perfect, spotless, sacrifice.

"Jesus said to him, "I am the way, and the truth, and the life. No one comes to the Father except through me."

JOHN 14:6 ESV

In the Old Testament, people would annually sacrifice their purest lamb to God to cover their sins. The lamb would cover the sins of the individual for the previous year but for the following year, each person would carry the weight of their sin until the next sacrifice. The reason why our lives can become heavy is because sin is heavy. Sin leads to guilt, guilt leads to shame, and shame leads to death. The Good News is that Jesus loves us, and His blood cleanses us from all sin, shame, and guilt! Jesus says, *"My yoke is easy and my burden is light."* (MATTHEW 11:30)

"Then I saw a young Lamb standing in the middle of the throne, encircled by the four living creatures and the twenty-four elders. He appeared to have been slaughtered but was now alive!"

REVELATION 5:6 TPT

Jesus sacrificed His life to set us free. We were bound by death but Jesus has given us life, through the resurrection. Now we can live completely free from fear of the future, free from all heaviness, and free from guilt and shame. We can live righteously, apart from sin, because Jesus has brought us into right standing with Father God.

Peace

"I leave the gift of peace with you—my peace. Not the kind of fragile peace given by the world, but my perfect peace. Don't yield to fear or be troubled in your hearts—instead, be courageous!"

JOHN 14:27 TPT

Peace is something the world is desperately searching for. The peace that Jesus gives is readily available and constant. The peace the world offers dissipates quickly while still leaving a void. A perfect example of this is drugs. You do it because you feel empty inside then it becomes a constant cycle of placing something in you that doesn't last forever. Some may say, "Well I've never done drugs." That may be true, but you don't have to do drugs to have an addiction. We can become addicted to money, food, clothes or even a particular lifestyle, where there's never enough. We never feel like we are enough because we never have enough. The peace that Jesus places in us last forever. Our hope and peace is found in Christ alone. A peace that ushers in life, healing, and wholeness. What the world needs is an encounter with Jesus Christ! How will they encounter Him? Through us! We are the hands and feet of Jesus, we are the carriers of His presence! We say, "There has to be something more!" And we are right, but the more we're longing for is not found in the world, it's found in Jesus!

"The thief comes only to steal and kill and destroy. I came that they may have life and have it abundantly."

JOHN 10:10 ESV

Jesus promises to give us abundant life! All of His promises are a firm foundation we can stand on with complete confidence! Scripture says that all of God's promises are yes and amen! If He said it, He will do it! A great example of this is God's promise to Noah thousands of years ago after the flood! To this day, we still see the fulfillment of God's promise to Noah. God gives us rainbows to remind us of this promise that He will never flood the earth again. If God's promises remain, so does He. Jesus' name is also referred to in Scripture as Immanuel which means, "God with us." Jesus has never left us nor forsaken us and He never will. Did you know that Jesus is also referred to as the Prince of Peace? (ISAIAH 9:6)

We have the Prince of Peace inside each of us so we, as carriers of peace, can release the peace of God everywhere we go! Now is the time for us to stop listening to the lies of fear and failure. Now is the time for us to start ushering in an encounter with Jesus to everyone around us. Everyone says they want to change the world but are we willing to pay the price? Are we willing to lay down our own agendas and plans? Are we willing to yield to the Father's perfect plan? Are we ready to walk with a yes in our spirits regardless of the cost? This is what it will take to reveal and release encounters with the one true living God to a lost world! We have to step out of this complacent, mundane lifestyle, and we have to step into a lifestyle of radical obedience to fulfill this mandate. As we live in the place of intimacy with Jesus, what we carry will manifest to those around us in the form of encounters and they will experience true peace and joy!

Joy

"These things I have spoken to you, that my joy may be in you, and that your joy may be full."

JOHN 15:11 ESV

In the natural, relationships often desire affirmation, encouragement and love. No one wants a relationship that is forced or harmful. We all desire a relationship that is healthy, pure, and real. Jesus is a gentleman and never forces us into a relationship with Him! The Father's desire is not to take anything from us but to fill us to overflowing within the relationship. The love Jesus has for us is unconditional and selfless, nothing can ever separate us from His love. This love doesn't cast a spotlight on our past failures or mistakes, rather, His love cascades like a waterfall and washes all of our sins away. The Father's love never stops chasing us down.

"With joy and gladness they are led along as they enter the palace of the king."

PSALMS 45:15 ESV

A common issue people run into is longing to be filled with more of Jesus but coming to Him with a cup that is already full. We can fill our cup with ourselves and leave no room for Jesus. If we aren't careful our lives can be filled with the circumstances that we face rather than being filled with the solution to life; Jesus. (JOHN 14:6) It's like somebody pouring hot coffee into a cup of cold coffee, it would taste disgusting because it would be lukewarm. Jesus said he'd rather us be hot or cold than for us to be lukewarm. (REVELATION 3:15-16)

Jesus isn't looking to pour more of Himself into a person that is already full. If we try to live like we have everything figured out then we will live with no room for the Holy Spirit to come in and lead us. However, when we walk in humility, with open hearts and surrendered lives, Jesus will come possess us with His love. In order to experience true joy, we must surrender this life to

Jesus. We must allow the Holy Spirit to come in and wreck our lives so that we can live in the abundant life He has for us!

The experience of a joy that is bubbling over comes when we not only are surrendered to Jesus, but when we also are secure in the love God. Consistency will enable this type of security. The love of Jesus is constant, so when that comes alive within us there will be an unwavering confidence that fills our hearts. Surrender is not just confound within a moment but it is a daily decision to give Jesus our lives. The moment we give ourselves fully away to Jesus, we will rest in the reality of the Father's love for us and those around us. This act of obedience will empower us to reveal to others the simplicity of receiving Jesus and living in His Kingdom. Now is the time to go back to the simplicity of the Gospel of Jesus Christ.

The Simplicity Of The Gospel

What is the Gospel?

"I can testify that the Word is true and deserves to be received by all, for Jesus Christ came into the world to bring sinners back to life—even me, the worst sinner of all!"

1 TIMOTHY 1:15 TPT

The Gospel of Jesus Christ is the revelation of Jesus' suffering and love for the individual. The Gospel begins within an individual and then is commissioned to the masses. We must first receive the revelation of the Gospel for ourselves before we can release it to others! It is from our mouths that we confess but it's from our heart that we believe.

"because, if you confess with your mouth that Jesus is Lord and believe in your heart that God raised him from the dead, you will be saved."

ROMANS 10:9 ESV

Our beliefs are revealed by the way we live. How can others see that Jesus actually saved us if our lives don't represent who Jesus is? The comfortable Gospel won't save us, it will only keep us stuck. In order for the world to encounter Jesus they have to see Jesus. When we represent Jesus well, we will see lives shift into their original purpose. We cannot allow fear and obligation to be the motivation with which we run to Jesus, but rather our motivation must be pure love and a desperate need for His presence.

"Those who are well have no need of a physician, but those who are sick. Go and learn what this means: 'I desire mercy, and not sacrifice.' For I came not to call the righteous, but sinners."

MATTHEW 9:12-13 ESV

The Gospel is received when we obtain the revelation of how much Jesus loves us. Out of His love, births our need for His mercy and grace. The Gospel is released when we realize that it is only in Jesus that we can truly live, move, and have our being! The simplicity of the Gospel is this, that the Father's love never stops running us down; that through Jesus' sacrifice, the Father now offers everyone new life!

Now, we have the opportunity to live in new life. We have to step into the Kingdom of God, where we carry a level of simplicity that can be obtained and carried by everyone who hears the call.

QUESTIONS

1. How can we portray the true image of Jesus in our daily lives?

2. What does returning to simplicity look like?

3. What is the kingdom of God made up of? How does this change our daily life?

4. Why is it vitally important to surrender?

5. What is the simplicity of the Gospel? How can you share it today?

CHAPTER TWO

Breaking The Mold

Every time we break through the mold, something breaks off of us. It's like a baby chick hatching from its egg. As it breaks through the mold of the egg, it realizes there's more to the world than it had ever known or experienced. In the same way, when we break through the spiritual mold in our life, we will get a deeper revelation of Jesus and step into a greater dimension of freedom. Jesus died so that we would not just know him, but live in complete freedom.

"So if the Son makes you free, then you are unquestionably free."

JOHN 8:36 AMP

Breaking The Mindset

What happens when a mindset gets in the way of knowing Jesus? It's easy to think we know Jesus because we have received him. However, I am willing to say, if we've been in any type of relationship, we haven't completely known the other person. For example, I married my wife because I love her but I am still learning new things about her. In the same way, just because we have chosen to be connected to Jesus doesn't mean we know Jesus intimately. Do we know Jesus or have we just been introduced to Him? Sadly, many people claim to know Jesus but have only been introduced to Him. We can say that Jesus is our Lord, but our relationship with Jesus cannot rest on the backs of others. We can't supplement the entirety of our relationship with podcasts, videos, blogs and various books and never engage and meet with Jesus ourselves. Connection reveals a level of confidence in the relationship but not the depth of the relationship. Just because I say I'm married, doesn't mean I instantly know everything about my wife. When we come to know Jesus intimately, our whole lives will be transformed and with each encounter with Jesus our lives will reveal more of Jesus. This is an invitation into deeper intimacy with Jesus. Depth transforms us.

"Do not be conformed to this world, but be transformed by the renewal of your mind, that by testing you may discern what is the will of God, what is good and acceptable and perfect."
ROMANS 12:2 ESV

Depth also gives us something the world cannot give us, longevity. When we step into the place of greater intimacy with Jesus, that place of confidence and trust, we are given access to new depths. There are two reasons why people have shallow relationships: a lack of hunger and a lack of confidence. When a couple stops learning about each other, they become disengaged in each other's lives. In the same way, when a couple lacks confidence in their love for each other, the relationship becomes rocky and on edge. Likewise, in our relationship with Jesus, without hunger, we will live disengaged from the presence of Jesus and without confidence, we will crumble under the pressures of life; no peace. Every relationship requires depth in order to have longevity. We must hunger to know and encounter more of Jesus and pair it with a confidence in Jesus' neverending affection for us. Then, as we encounter Jesus with a confidence in His neverending affection for us, our thoughts will manifest heavenly realities.

"Yes, feast on all the treasures of the heavenly realm and fill your thoughts with heavenly realities, and not with the distractions of the natural realm."

COLOSSIANS 3:2 TPT

A wise old man once told me, "If you don't learn, you won't grow." Sometimes, even the good things of this earth can prevent us from accessing the greater realities. When we become comfortable with the good, we'll have no need to seek after the greater. A deep relationship with Jesus is a constant journey of hungering for more, learning the realities of Jesus and exploding in growth! This means we must position our hearts to be open and receive even when we don't understand, we have to have a teachable spirit. A teachable spirit will reveal both our confidence and our trust in the nature of who God is.

Breaking Off Religion

There's a difference between religion and relationship. In the Old Testament, religion consisted of the Law and the prophets, where God directed and redirected His people back to His heart so they could encounter His presence. However, in the New Testament, Jesus fulfilled both the Law and the prophets, ushering in the opportunity for a relationship, where God's presence lives in and among His people. Religion that is dangerous is religion that removes relationship by carrying a lack of transparency. Within the mold of religion is self promotion. It's often more about self then it is about anyone else. We have to be willing to look beyond ourselves; our experience, our knowledge and our reasoning. Religion is like putting on noise canceling headphones, it isolates and shuts off everything around us so that the spotlight is solely on us, instead of on Jesus.

Jesus gives us a revelation of this with the example of the Pharisees.

"Everything they do is done for show and to be noticed by others."

MATTHEW 23:5 TPT

For this reason alone, Jesus can be right in front of our eyes and we can miss Him entirely. Jesus wept over the death of his friend Lazarus, but did you know that Jesus also wept over a people who missed their visitation? (LUKE 19:41-44) When our attention is fixated on ourselves instead of being present with His presence, we miss our visitation with Jesus. We will expound more on the reality of staying present in *Chapter Six: There Is More*. When we allow our attention to be disfigured through the situations of life, we'll respond from a perspective that is consistent with being outside of relationship. This doesn't mean our response removes our relationship, it simply means we have the option to respond from a place of emptiness or a place of fulfillment. The relationship with Jesus is not only a place of fulfillment but the relationship also forms as a conduit of visitation with Jesus.

Recognizing and engaging in a visitation from Jesus is crucial as we walk in relationship with Him. Jesus wants us to encounter Him through various avenues, such as, through Scripture. Jesus is more eager to meet with you than you are to meet with Him.

3 Dimensions of Scripture

When we read Scripture we not only have the opportunity to receive a visitation from Jesus, but we also have the ability to access new dimensions within the encounter with Jesus.

The first dimension of Scripture is where we engage in the historical, scientific and factual aspects of Scripture; what I call the *mind level*. This dimension is good for gathering the context in which a particular passage or book was written. However, only engaging in the first dimension of Scripture will render us to a position of only knowing about Jesus but never truly engaging in the relationship with Jesus. When we no longer engage in the relationship with Jesus, we will slip slowly into religiosity. We can know what Jesus said and did, but never allow Jesus' words and actions to penetrate deep within our hearts and permeate in our lives. We have to move beyond knowing about the historical Jesus and engage into knowing the person Jesus.

The second dimension of Scripture is where we engage certain verses or passages based on current circumstances or situations. This is what I call the *heart level*. Many times, God will speak through Scripture to reveal the reality of His presence in our particular predicament. Engaging His presence within Scripture will empower our spirits to be directed and redirect into His strength. The Lord's strength is always the solution to our weakness. When we engage proactively in the presence of Jesus, within Scripture, we will shift from just knowing facts about Jesus to knowing Jesus the person. The difference between the first and second dimension of Scripture, is the revelation of Jesus. One reveals Jesus as though He is a distant fictional character and the other reveals Jesus as a person who desires to become more real than anything else in our lives. Our hearts will overflow with the reality of Jesus when we embrace intimacy with the person Jesus.

The third dimension of Scripture is where we commune with Jesus; what I believe is the *spirit level*. This dimension opens as our love relationship with Jesus deepens in intimacy and our spirit man intertwines with the Spirit of the Living God. As we engage in the third dimension of Scripture, our spirit man is consumed in the intimate thoughts and emotions of the Lord. Our spirit man must be consumed in the Lord; rest in His nature. If we stop becoming dependent on Jesus, we will slowly slip into a lesser intimacy and eventually be entangled in passivity. The Father is looking for a people to commune with.

TESTIMONY

One evening at a youth service in South Africa, I was asked to minister to the students and the Lord began touching everyone in the room. The following night, there was a specific testimony that began circulating. The night before as the Lord was touching us, a seven year old boy came forward and was impacted heavily by the Lord. The young boy was instantly taken into a vision. This is his own account witnessed and approved by his family:

"I saw a man standing in front of me and the man said, "I am God." The man had long hair with a beard. He took my hand and walked with me. He stretched out His hand and asked me to walk with Him. God showed me that I am one of His shepherds. God walked with me and showed me what happened between David and Goliath, what happened in the lion's den and who the Israelites were." The most amazing thing of all, after the family had suffered such great loss, God took the young boy's hand and turned him around. The Lord showed him his grandmother and said, "Your grandmother is here with me and she is waiting for you."

Visitations aren't birthed out of the hunger for a visitation. Visitations are birthed out of the hunger for more of Jesus. There is a call for us to be present with Jesus moment by moment; turning our attention to Him and allowing the Holy Spirit to access and flow into every area of our lives. Allowing Jesus to permeate in every area of our lives will break every ounce of religion off of us. Religion wants to box us in but God wants us to break out.

"Now the Lord is the Spirit, and where the Spirit of the Lord is, there is freedom."

2 CORINTHIANS 3:17 ESV

Breaking Off The Flesh

Our flesh is the very thing that seeks to provoke us in disengaging from the relationship with Jesus and living the Spirit-filled life. Romans tells us that, *"Those who are motivated by the flesh only pursue what benefits themselves. But those who live by the impulses of the Holy Spirit are motivated to pursue spiritual realities."* (Romans 8:5 TPT) Later, Scripture continues to describe this war between the flesh and the Spirit. *"In fact, the mind-set focused on the flesh fights God's plan and refuses to submit to his direction, because it cannot!"* (Romans 8:7 TPT) The flesh pursues the desires of the flesh and the spirit pursues the desires of the Spirit. Without yielding to the Spirit, our flesh cannot submit to God. If we want Jesus to permeate in every area of our lives, we have to yield to the Holy Spirit everyday and allow Him to take control of our lives; breaking off every desire of the flesh.

Choosing Jesus is beautiful, yet often overlooked due to the passiveness in our hearts. We will shout for Jesus to save us, but do we ever truly desire for Jesus to take control of us? "Well, it'll looks funny" and "they'll call me crazy." Who cares? Is Jesus worth it? Jesus' blood covers us and His life sacrificed on the cross saves us. Where is the fruit on our trees that grows as a result of being saved by Jesus? Fruit only comes through the Holy Spirit.

We must allow the Holy Spirit to take complete control of our life. True freedom is only deposited and received through relationship with the Holy Spirit. It's time for us to break out! We need the Holy Spirit to break our mindset, break off religiosity and break off our flesh, so that we can step into who God has called us to be.

"And we all, with unveiled face, beholding the glory of the Lord, are being transformed into the same image from one degree of glory to another. For this comes from the Lord who is the Spirit."

2 CORINTHIANS 3:18 ESV

QUESTIONS

1. Why is depth important to our relationship?

2. What type of spirit reveals both our confidence and trust in the nature of God?

3. What is religion? Relationship? How can we shift into relationship?

4. Describe each of the three dimensions of Scripture.

5. What does it look like to allow the Holy Spirit to take control of our life?

CHAPTER THREE

Capturing The Heart

The heart is a peculiar organ. Much like other organs, the heart is unseen. What is intriguing is that the heart is the only organ that can tangibly be felt throughout areas of the body. The heart pumps blood through the body creating a pulse-like sensation. We don't have to feel the heartbeat to know we are alive, but we do have to be alive to feel a heartbeat.

Jesus desires for our lives to be in sync with His heartbeat. If we want the heartbeat of Heaven, we have to touch the heart of God and allow our heart to be recalibrated to His.

The Heart Of Jesus

The heart of Jesus is for His life to reveal the Father. From the gracious love of the Father, that rushes through the veins of the Son, transferred into us, our hearts will come in sync with the Heavenly realm. The heart of Jesus is ever present and forever constant. His love remains in a constant state of steadfast pursuit of you and I. (PSALM 136) The heart of Jesus is like a train that will never be derailed. His pursuit is not for those who have no need, but for those who realize their need for Him. Jesus wants people who need Him. The people who will hunger for more. The more is always found in Jesus Christ. There's no other place. You can search all over this world and you will never find anyone else like

Jesus. Even the greatest wonders of this world fail in comparison to Jesus. His righteousness is taller than any mountain, His judgment deeper than any sea, His love reaches to the Heavens and His mercy knows no limits. The grace of God is endless, and His love is steadfast.

There's no one like Jesus. Jesus, who carried the perfect nature of God and gave Himself away for us. Our Savior, treated as though He was a robber, robbed the grave so we can live. To live in the heartbeat of Jesus, what a beautiful thing.

The Father's heart is positioned to be in fellowship with a holy people; a Jesus centered people. A Jesus centered people are those whose lifestyle consist of being caught up in the Spirit and carry the residue of the Truth. (JOHN 4:23-24) Jesus wants a bride to commune with. Jesus will never stop pursuing intimacy with us.

The heartbeat of Jesus is His love rushing in to meet us and for our love to minister back to Him. Loving Jesus is not based on being inwardly focused nor on our performance. Too often I allowed my performance to dictate my relationship with Jesus. If I didn't perform well, then my relationship wasn't going well. My performance doesn't make me healthy, Jesus does. Jesus isn't looking for a performance, he's looking for our obedience. Will we fall in love with Jesus? Jesus didn't come and ask for a spotless bride, He came and made a spotless bride. Jesus isn't looking for performers, He's looking for lovers. Will we allow Jesus to love us? He's waiting on us. He's not asking what more we can do, He is simply waiting to marry us. Will we be radical lovers of Jesus?

"How could you worship two gods at the same time? You will have to hate one and love the other, or be devoted to one and despise the other. You can't worship the true God while enslaved to the god of money."

MATTHEW 6:24 TPT

The hunger for more is found when our love transcends this world and is fully positioned on Jesus.

The Heart Of People

Our desire to carry the heartbeat of Jesus, must receive an installment of radical love and forgiveness. It seems we find the greatest difficulty when someone close hurts us. How do we move forward and still love them well? Conveniently enough, Jesus had a disciple named Judas who would betray Him. This is how Scripture describes Jesus, in full knowledge of the betrayal, before the one who would betray Him;

"Jesus knew that the night before Passover would be his last night on earth before leaving this world to return to the Father's side. All throughout his time with his disciples, Jesus had demonstrated a deep and tender love for them. And now he longed to show them the full measure of his love. Before their evening meal had begun, the accuser had already planted betrayal into the heart of Judas Iscariot, the son of Simon. Now Jesus was fully aware that the Father had placed all things under his control, for he had come from God and was about to go back to be with him. So he got up from the meal and took off his outer robe, and took a towel and

wrapped it around his waist. Then he poured water into a basin and began to wash the disciples' dirty feet and dry them with his towel."

JOHN 13:1-5 TPT

Jesus was not interested in making a scene, He was interested in giving us an example of how to pursue love, even in the midst of our greatest circumstances. Jesus not only continued to love the people who hurt Him, He found an opportunity to serve them. When we choose to serve and bless the people who have hurt us, we will be operating in the radical love of the Father.

"But I say to you who hear, Love your enemies, do good to those who hate you, bless those who curse you, pray for those who abuse you."

LUKE 6:27-28 ESV

How Blessing Will Change You

1. Find the good in that person and mediaite on His goodness within them.

When we begin to actively seek out the good within people who have wronged us, our hearts will shift into the Father's reality; seeing the way the Father sees. We will then begin to receive the installment of Jesus' heart. The installment of Jesus' heart will take us further in His love. We must positively meditate on the goodness of God within each person.

2. Thank God for the good He has placed within them.

As we positively meditate on that person's success, begin to erupt in thanksgiving to God for His design and His goodness within that person.

3. Ask God to bless them in specific areas.

Out of thanking God for that person and the qualities or virtue they possess, begin genuinely asking God to bless them in specific areas of their life. (finances, health, family, job, etc.)

4. Bless them in such a tangible way that it seems ridiculous.

Find a way to tangibly bless the particular person who may have said or done something wrong against you. As you move in this wave of generosity, bless this person beyond what you would normally do for yourself or anyone else. This act of love will shift us from just praying blessings, to proactively living as true sons of God. When we move in radical forgiveness, radical love will manifest.

Radical forgiveness is the product of radical love. We have to access radical love and allow it to possess every area of our lives. Radical love will manifest when we are confident and secure in our love relationship with Jesus. The only way we become confident and secure in our love relationship is by receiving what the Father says about us. Jesus knows what's within each of us, especially the good that we can often overlook. Jesus knew that Judas (Jesus' financial administrator / treasurer) was stealing money from His ministry and that

Judas would later betray Him. Inspite of this, Jesus never nurtured resentment. Radical love manifested in the life of Jesus because Jesus was secure in the love relationship with His Father. Jesus allowed radical forgiveness to flow out of the love relationship He shared with the Father. The result of operating in radical love is the birth of mindblowing, wall breaking forgiveness.

"For if you forgive others their trespasses [their reckless and willful sins], your heavenly Father will also forgive you. But if you do not forgive others [nurturing your hurt and anger with the result that it interferes with your relationship with God], then your Father will not forgive your trespasses."

MATTHEW 6:14-15 AMP

When we choose to operate in the radical forgiveness that transcends our fleshly behaviors, we will see a greater love for people than we've ever seen before. Jesus didn't just teach it, He lived it. Jesus doesn't command us to do something that He doesn't already set the example of. "Well, I'm not Jesus." Jesus is fully God and fully man. Jesus felt the same pull of emotions that we do. "Well, it's difficult." Jesus didn't say it would be easy, He simply set the example of what is possible. (MARK 10:27)

The Father is looking for us to carry the heart of Jesus so that the hearts of people will shift into the reality of who Jesus is. The Father is first interested in our hearts receiving the installment of Jesus' heart. Our hearts will be transformed into Jesus' heart when our eyes lock with His eyes and our eyes become His eyes.

When we can see people the way the Jesus sees us, then we can love people the way the Father loves. We have to love the way the Father loves us. We have to see through the Father's eyes to grasp the love He desires for us to transfer to others.

The Heart Of Self

Jesus Christ died for the sins of the world, but you and I kept him up on the cross. Scripture says,

"Do you think that I cannot appeal to my Father, and he will at once send me more than twelve legions of angels?"

MATTHEW 26:53 ESV

It is my personal belief that when Jesus died on the cross, He saw our faces and said "You're worth it, I'll stay a little longer." Jesus believed we were worth dying for. But do we have that same love for one another?

We can't love the way Jesus loves until we get a revelation of the way Jesus loves us. If we can see ourselves through the eyes of Jesus, then we'll overflow with love for others. Love without Jesus is conditional, but love in Jesus is unconditional. The love of Jesus has no limitations and is not bound by restrictions. Jesus' heart is for us to encounter the depths of His love, including His love sacrifice.

"For the greatest love of all is a love that sacrifices all. And this great love is demonstrated when a person sacrifices his life for his friends."

JOHN 15:13 TPT

Jesus longs for us as sons and daughters to walk in His loving presence; to thrive in life, not just to survive. Jesus died to give us new life, not for us to live in the old one. The reason why we often feel like we're just surviving is because we're trying to do things we used to do and not stepping into the new. It's like a caterpillar that has gone through metamorphosis and has been transformed into a butterfly. The butterfly cannot go back into the cocoon but instead, it launches out, transformed into the more. The old cannot fit in the new. Old routines won't work and the old lifestyle has to die.

Jesus' love sacrifice transforms our lives for a purpose. When we live transformed lives, we will become those who transform rather than those who conform. Jesus desires to reveal, not only the reality of His love for us, but the reality of our destiny.

QUESTIONS

1. What does it look like to be Jesus centered?

2. What are some ways you can bless those who have wronged you?

3. How does radical love manifest? Ask the Father what He thinks about you.

4. What does a transformed life look like?

CHAPTER FOUR

Redefining & Discovering You

Life's moments are compiled into two categories: moments where we succeed and the moments that carry the opportunity to learn. Often, our response to failure determines our perception on our identity and our destiny. Jesus Christ died on the cross so that our spirit would shift into the reality of what is and not what was. We are found when we lose ourselves to the reality of Jesus' love for us. Everything that couldn't move suddenly moves. Every impossibility becomes possible. But often times our earthly realm of intellect prohibits the realm of possibility. We catch ourselves saying, "I've gone too far for God to accept me." "I've done too much for God to forgive me." "No one truly loves me." "I'm all alone." Each of these statements are lies that are designed to create confusion in the knowledge of the Father's voice. A lie's purpose is to simply implant a false reality on the divine design that has been placed within you. Every lie seeks to undermine the significance of our identity, our purpose and our destiny. The truth is birthed from intimacy with Jesus.

Breaking Off The Lies

These "IN's" want to establish lies in us and end us.

3 IN's That Undermine Significance

1. The Lie Of Inadequacy

One of the biggest questions a person faces in life is, "Who am I?" This question can often be provoked out of a lack of intimacy or a thought of inadequacy. Inadequacy often rises out of a place where we perceive that we aren't good enough or we don't have what it takes. Inadequacy simply wants to implant insecurity in our identity. Fortunately, this deception has a line of origin. The devil is desperate to destroy our identity because if we know who we are and know what the Father says about us, then we will become secure in our design. We won't entertain insecurity through the envy of others, but we'll be confident in the established work of the cross. True security in our identity is a reflection that we are operating as true sons and daughters of the Living God. Our identity mirrors who we belong to.

In the beginning, the devil spoke to the woman and said, *"Did God actually say, 'You shall not eat of any tree in the garden'?""* (GENESIS 3:1) And then he later says, *"You will not surely die. For God knows that when you eat of it your eyes will be opened, and you will be like God, knowing good and evil."* (GENESIS 3:5-6) What's interesting, is Adam and Eve were already like God. Previously, God spoke over them and said, *"Let us make man in our image, after our likeness."* (GENESIS 1:26) And then the Lord commanded them not to eat of the tree of the knowledge of good and evil. (GENESIS 2:16-17) The devil first provoked the woman to question what God spoke over them. Once manipulated, mankind responded out of insecurity regarding their identity. Our identity is hidden within the design. The same God who

45

spoke creation into existence, deposited our identity into the depths of our being. We have a choice to either live and respond from His image or live and respond out of insecurity.

It's not surprising that the devil's first initial attack against humanity was against identity. Identity births security and security in Jesus produces power. Our identity has power. Another place we see an attack against identity is when satan tries try to manipulate Jesus into a place of responding from insecurity. *"And the tempter came and said to him, "If you are the Son of God, command these stones to become loaves of bread.""* (MATTHEW 4:3) Notice that the Father's deposit of identity preceded the trial. *"and behold, a voice from heaven said, "This is my beloved Son, with whom I am well pleased.""* (MATTHEW 3:17)

The Lord will not allow us to be tempted or tested in an area that He hasn't already spoken into. The Father's desire is for us to hear His heart so that we may be able to distinguish between the lies. When we walk with sensitivity to the Father's voice, security and confidence of our identity in Christ is released. True identity is released when we embrace the revelation that we are adopted into the family of God and we are embraced as His sons and daughters. Just as a father and mother's DNA is implanted into their child, so our Heavenly Father implants His DNA in us. We carry the characteristics of God because we are made in His image. (GENESIS 1:27) There is nothing else on planet earth that can match our design because our design is specific to the individual. Since we are made in His image, then it's plausible to wonder, "What does He look like?" Jesus said, *"Whoever has seen me has seen the Father."* (JOHN 14:9) Let's take a deeper look into Jesus:

"In the beginning was the Word, and the Word was with God, and the Word was God. He was in the beginning with God. All things were made through him, and without him was not any thing made that was made. In him was life, and the life was the light of men. The light shines in the darkness, and the darkness has not overcome it."

JOHN 1:1-5 ESV

Everything was made through Jesus; the living Word. Jesus, born of a virgin, came into the world as a man and lived a sinless life. Jesus faced the same difficulties we face, yet prevailed without sin. When we accept Jesus Christ as Lord, Jesus reconciles us back to the Father and restores us to our original design in the Father's eyes. The original design is walking with the Lord in complete righteousness and communion; our attention intimately fixed on His goodness.

2. The Lie Of Being Ineffective

This profound yet simple revelation of our identity will catapult us into a level of security. The goal, however, is not to just to be secure in our identity but to be proactive in our purpose. "What's my purpose?" Purpose is revealed from our security in the Lord. When we carry a level of confidence in the Lord, we will access the realms of possibility and discover that which supersedes our own personal agenda. When we discover our true

47

purpose, lies will try to distract from the security in our identity and project failures before we even begin. Ineffectual lies seek to implant thoughts of being unqualified and even to have a fear of being ineffective. This lie's main purpose is to paralyze us into a place of not wanting to disappoint so that we do nothing. The revelation of eternal value will help propel us into our purpose. Each of us has value and what we have in us has eternal value. We need to uncover and step into the value that's been placed inside of us. Everyone brushes against their purpose daily, but through Christ, we have the opportunity to discover our multi-layered purpose.

Multi-Layered Purpose

Layer 1: The Purpose Of My Today.

"You saw who you created me to be before I became me! Before I'd ever seen the light of day, the number of days you planned for me were already recorded in your book."

PSALMS 139:16 TPT

Every day has purpose. Our purpose is embedded within the day, waiting for us to access and grab hold of it. The world is looking for more than an acknowledgement but an action. The purpose of each of our days are multi-dimensional and are faceted with various reactions yet the core of each day is to simply reveal Jesus. Jesus calls us to be a witness for him to the ends of the earth. (ACTS 1:8) Lives don't change solely on our own but rather through Jesus Christ in us.

If people only see us, nothing happens. But if the world encounters Jesus through us, everything changes.

Layer 2: The Purpose Of Life.

"You even formed every bone in my body when you created me in the secret place, carefully, skillfully shaping me from nothing to something."
PSALMS 139:15 TPT

Look around you. Life is moving. It's in the sway of the trees, the force of the bird's wings and even in the ever changing canvas of the sky. Life is all around us and every day we live in it. But what's the purpose of life? We have to look beyond ourselves and look at life as a whole; the big picture. Life is marvelously beautiful because Scripture declares that creation magnifies the Creator; it can't help but glorify Him.

"Let the heavens be glad, and let the earth rejoice; let the sea roar, and all that fills it; let the field exult, and everything in it! Then shall all the trees of the forest sing for joy before the Lord, for he comes, for he comes to judge the earth. He will judge the world in righteousness and the peoples in his faithfulness."
PSALMS 96:11-13 ESV

Even Jesus said, *"If my followers were silenced, the very stones would break forth with praises!"* (LUKE

19:40) The purpose of life is to simply be present in the presence of the Lord and to glorify Him.

"Let everything that has breath praise the Lord! Praise the Lord!"

PSALMS 150:6 ESV

Layer 3: The Purpose Of Why I Was Created.

"You formed my innermost being, shaping my delicate inside and my intricate outside, and wove them all together in my mother's womb. I thank you, God, for making me so mysteriously complex! Everything you do is marvelously breathtaking. It simply amazes me to think about it! How thoroughly you know me, Lord!"

PSALMS 139:13-14 TPT

"Why was I created?" This is a question that many people ask and then dismiss because of the headache that follows. Living life in the mundane either hardens us to spiritual realities or we become desperately hungry for more. Will we search the depth to discover our greatest reality? Jesus knew why He was put on this earth. (JOHN 17) Jesus fulfilled His purpose because He knew His destiny. We will fulfill our purpose when we are no longer entertained by the thought nor when our heart's desire is to entertain a crowd, but when our attention is fixed on Jesus.

Purpose was never designed to operate as leverage but was always designed for relationship. If we become so focused that we isolate ourselves and miss people, we will miss our purpose. We were always created to operate in a purpose that goes beyond ourselves. Purpose isn't isolating nor does it rely solely on the individual. Purpose was never meant to stay in you but was always meant to flow through you. We will live on purpose, when we live by His Word and by His promises.

Identifying Our Calling

3 Principles Of New Covenant Calling

1.The Lord breathes the calling within the individual.

2.Someone may prophesy (forthtelling / foretelling) the calling.

3.The calling is birthed within the individual.

The Lord is seeking to breathe a call within each of His children. Just as an earthly father will speak the untamed potential over His child, so the Father desires to breathe a call, within His children, that contains the unlimited raw potential of His nature. Every father desires to see their child look like them and every good father desires to see their child achieve unmatched success. The Father loves to brag about His children.

There are many ways we see the Lord breathe a calling; **dreams** (GENESIS 37:5-9 & GENESIS 45:1-11), **visions** (ACTS 18:5-11), **visitations** (ACTS 26:12-18), **angels** (LUKE 1:26-38), **creation** (JONAH 1:4-15 & 3:1-10), **trances** (ACTS 10:9-48) **prophetic acts** (JUDGES 6:11-23, 36-40) and through the **Word of God**

51

(2 TIMOTHY 3:16-17) . Each of these are not only ways that the Lord breathes our calling but are also ways He continually speaks to us today. Jesus wants a personal connection so that it's not us trying to communicate with Him, hoping for a response, but Jesus wants to communicate back and forth with us. The Father wants what He breathed into us to be birthed within us so that we will confidently and boldly step into our destiny.

To give some insight of prophecy, Scripture reveals to us two forms of prophecy; forthtelling and foretelling. *Forthtelling* is the prophetic word that calls someone or something to be. A biblical example of this would be where God spoke to Ezekiel to prophesy to the dry bones to come alive, and they did. (EZEKIEL 1:1-14) We have the honor to prophesy the Father's heart over people and call them to step into who they are in His eyes. It's the goodness of God that leads us to repentance. (ROMANS 2:4) When we call forth the good that has been placed within each person from the beginning, we will see lives radically altered into the image of Jesus. The other form of prophecy is foretelling. *Foretelling* is the prophetic word that reveals a measure of the future. A wonderful biblical example of foretelling is Agabus prophesied a famine coming to the world and out of this prophetic word the church having the ability to prepare in advance. (ACTS 11:27-30) Through the Spirit, we all have access to benefit one another, in love, by the gifts that help build our faith.

"So with yourselves, since you are eager for manifestations of the Spirit, strive to excel in building up the church."

1 CORINTHIANS 14:12 ESV

Biblically Identifying The Principles

To help us identify the principles of new covenant calling, we will navigate through the lives of New Testament persons who encountered the person Jesus and whose calling radically altered the direction of history. Our calling will not only alter the direction of our lives but our calling also has the mass potential to alter the course of history.

All things have been made by Jesus and through Jesus, including the revelation of calling. The revelation of calling first originates with Jesus Christ our Lord.

Since Jesus is our example, then it would make sense for us to first identify these principles in His calling. We first see **the Lord breathe** Jesus' calling into being, through an *angel*, to Jesus' earthly parents. (MATTHEW 1:18-25 & LUKE 1:26-38) Later, Jesus is presented in the temple and Simeon, with the Holy Spirit upon him, **prophesies** (*foretelling*) the calling of Jesus; to bring salvation for all peoples. (LUKE 2:25-35) After this, the child Jesus grew and begin to grasp His destiny. (LUKE 2:41-52) Jesus' calling is **birthed** when Jesus, in the power of the Holy Spirit, confidently steps out of the test and into His ministry. (LUKE 4:14-15) Tests will provide the opportunity for confidence, in His love, to be built up. The power of the Holy Spirit will manifest love to win.

The next calling we will navigate through is the calling of Peter, the disciple of Jesus. We see the Lord first **breathe** the reality of Peter's calling through the *prophetic act* of catching a large number of fish; their

53

nets began breaking and their boats began to sink. (LUKE 5:1-7) Then we see Jesus **prophesy** (*forthtelling*) Peter's calling, as a fisher of men. (MATTHEW 4:18-20, MARK 1:16-18 & LUKE 5:8-11) Throughout the Gospels, we can see the ministry of the apostles. However, I believe we see a clear picture of Peter's **calling birthed** at Pentecost when about three thousand responded to the Good News of Jesus Christ. (ACTS 2:14-41) What's beautiful is that Peter went through a process of stepping into his calling; from the boat to Pentecost. Every calling must go through a process of testing, pruning and maturing. This process doesn't deactivate our calling, but instead the process reveals our true motives; producing the opportunity for us to be refined and released. This process will birth the purest form of calling and manifest with extraordinary results.

In the last calling, we will analyze the calling of the apostle Paul in the New Testament. We begin with Paul's (previously named Saul) vigorous effort to destroy the followers of Jesus Christ of Nazareth. On his way, on a road to Damascus, **the Lord breathes** Paul's calling through a *visitation*. (ACTS 26:12-18) Then, directly after the visitation, Paul becomes blind and led into the city of Damascus. We then see Ananias, directed by the Lord, to heal Paul and **prophesy** (*forthtelling*) his calling. (ACTS 9:10-18 & 22:12-16) We then see the calling within Paul **birthed** by the Lord supernaturally healing Paul from blindness, through Ananias. The calling birthed within Paul, manifested the confidence to rise up and become a disciple of Jesus. When our destiny becomes a reality, not through understanding but through faith, we will access a greater realm of obedience and confidence.

It's interesting that the enemy continuously opposes what the Lord has spoken over us and what He has designed us for. The question is, will we allow the Lord to breathe our calling within us, allowing the prophetic words to confirm and manifest God's design for us, so that our calling will be birthed within us? When our calling is birthed within us, then we become eligible to give birth to our destiny.

3. The Lie Of Insignificancy

In a big universe, it's not uncommon for us to question the value of our destiny. But what if it became common to see and recognize our eternal value and the value within others? Unfortunately, a lot of people have already made their conclusions regarding their destiny. "I can't make a difference" and "I'm not that important so why does it matter?" But the Father is saying something very different. "I've made you different so that my Son would make a difference through you." (JEREMIAH 1:5) People may have similar traits, but no one person has the exact combination of traits as another person. Before Jesus makes a difference through us, He wants to make a difference in us. (2 CORINTHIANS 3:18) It's easier for us to say that we want change than it is to allow change to get inside us. Saying aloud that we want change doesn't require sacrifice but the process of being changed does. If we want Jesus to make a difference through us, then the things that are preventing difference in us have to die. (MATTHEW 16:25) Many people say that one person can't make a difference but I know a man who changed the course of history and humanity in a singular moment. His name is Jesus Christ. When

people no longer see us but see Jesus, then all will
encounter the Difference Maker.

Who Will You Become?

Our lives have been re-written with the blood of Jesus.
When we step in, our whole world changes. We begin to
redefine ourselves through the eyes of Jesus and we
begin to discover that we were made for so much more.
Are you hungry for more?

QUESTIONS

1. How do we identify truth?

2. What does walking in our original design look like?

3. What is the purpose of today? What is the purpose of life?

4. How do we live on purpose? What are His promises?

5. Why does the Lord want to make a difference in us?

CHAPTER FIVE

Catch The Fire

We all want to burn for Jesus! But if we don't have the right structure, we'll be the ones that get burned. It's like building a bonfire. When there is too much structure, it won't catch fire. With the right amount of structure, the fire will last. My prayer is that you will catch fire and the fire will last!

When To Wait

It seems odd that we would be told to wait. This concept used to irk me. I would be extremely irritated by this concept because I felt like people were trying to put me down. What I discovered is that some people will dismiss you but others have a pure desire to see you burn for a lifetime.

A fire does more harm than good when it is out of control. But when the fire has proportioned structure, it warms all who come near. I believe, as we live a life that carries the fire of God with Holy Spirit-inspired structure, the Lord will brand people by fire through us. People will encounter the Father and tangibly experience the love of Jesus flowing through us.

Here are a few guidelines for proportional structure that will help the fire last:

The Need For Accountability

Having the right people around us is crucial to keep us from burning out. If we have people around us that aren't paying attention to what God wants to do, then we'll be too distracted to keep the fire going. We need people who will help build the fire with us and not let the fire die in us. Scripture says that bad company corrupts good morals. We must surround ourselves with people who throw jet fuel on our fire, not wet blankets!

This doesn't mean we stop witnessing to people who are different than us, it just means we run with a people that are heading in the same direction. When we think of Jesus we see there are layers of relationship. Jesus had the crowd, the twelve disciples, the three, and then John who laid his head upon Jesus' chest. We must follow this example! Not everyone is for our inner circle. We must guard our hearts, and make sure our inner circle is filled with people on fire! There is a difference between witnessing to and witnessing with. God's original intent was for us to commune with the Lord and be in fellowship with other people. Scripture says,

"Jesus answered him, 'Love the Lord your God with every passion of your heart, with all the energy of your being, and with every thought that is within you.' This is the great and supreme commandment. And the second is like it in importance: 'You must love your friend in the same way you love yourself.'"

MATTHEW 22:37-39 TPT

Communing with the Lord is vitally important and so is being in fellowship with other people. If we aren't in fellowship with other people, how then will we reveal to them the love of the Father? We have to commune with the Lord and allow His love to transfer through us to others. If we haven't received His love, we can't transfer His love.

The trap lies within the lie that since we've been hurt by people we can't associate or be around certain people. The Lord desires for us to be His witnesses throughout all of the world (ACTS 1:8), but we need people around us that are witnesses to the revelation of Jesus Christ.

It's easier to stand for something when there is a multitude of people in agreement in comparison to when it's just us. A lion will not typically attack an entire group of water buffalo, but instead it will pursue the straggler at the back of the pack or the one who has chosen to be disconnected from the herd. Walking in solitude is dangerous. There's wisdom in going to war with people who are walking in the same direction and who will stand with you. Accountability is not just there to keep us on course, but it is meant to help build each other up and keep the fire going within us.

"To each is given the manifestation of the Spirit for the common good."

1 CORINTHIANS 12:7 ESV

The Need For Alignment

We need people to keep us accountable, but we also need to be aligned. Alignment and accountability go hand and hand. When we have both elements in our life we will produce more fruit. Upon this, there is a difference between accountability and alignment.

Accountability is when people run together and together discover more of the Lord. These people make a priority of speaking the truth in love to those they are connected with. Likewise, the priority of alignment is oneness; pursuing oneness with each other and encouraging each other into oneness with Jesus. Within alignment, we receive transferable kingdom goods (wisdom, knowledge, impartation, etc.) that flow from the Father's heart. A biblical depiction of how alignment will transfer and flow kingdom goods into our lives is found in PSALM 133; the oil that ran down Aaron's beard. When we are in alignment we are able to receive extensive experience and various kingdom goods without a receipt. Some things cannot be bought but only received through a humble and teachable spirit. When we come into alignment, the people we align with have the authority to pour into us so that we have the opportunity to grow in the Spirit beyond your own natural ability. These are the spiritual fathers and mothers of the faith.

We need spiritual fathers and mothers. Elisha had Elijah, John the Beloved had Jesus and Timothy had Paul. All through Scripture, spiritual fathers would impart and download the things of God into the spiritual son.

Often times, the misconception is that a spiritual father lords over a spiritual son. Scripture declares that we are all one in Christ Jesus (ROMANS 12:5). Scripture also declares that we must submit to God (JAMES 4:7) and submit to each other out of reverence for Christ Jesus. (EPHESIANS 5:20-21) We submit to God and honor spiritual fathers and mothers. (EPHESIANS 6:1-3) [*/

61

believe this passage has the ability to pertain to both spiritual parents and earthly parents.]

Paul not only imparted things into Timothy (2 TIMOTHY 1:6-7), but Paul also gave us an example of how to truly father in the Spirit.

"For I long to see you, that I may impart to you some spiritual gift to strengthen you— that is, that we may be mutually encouraged by each other's faith, both yours and mine."

ROMANS 1:11-12 ESV

Fathering in the Spirit, is birthed out of a pure connection in the Spirit. A father and son long to be together, sharing in oneness and encouraging one another on into a greater knowledge of the Son. This is the Father's heart for His children. A father never fears for the success of a son, a father always beams with pride as his son shines and succeeds. Spiritual fathers will give their shoulders to step onto so that the spiritual son can reach higher and further than they could reach before. True spiritual fathers are submitted to the Father and send people out to fulfill their God-given assignment. The essence of alignment should be to encourage each other into oneness with the Father and Jesus Christ.

"And I ask not only for these disciples, but also for all those who will one day believe in me through their message. I pray for them all to be joined together as one even as you and I, Father, are joined together as one. I

pray for them to become one with us so that the world will recognize that you sent me. For the very glory you have given to me I have given them so that they will be joined together as one and experience the same unity that we enjoy. You live fully in me and now I live fully in them so that they will experience perfect unity, and the world will be convinced that you have sent me, for they will see that you love each one of them with the same passionate love that you have for me. "Father, I ask that you allow everyone that you have given to me to be with me where I am! Then they will see my full glory— the very splendor you have placed upon me because you have loved me even before the beginning of time. "You are my righteous Father, but the unbelieving world has never known you in the perfect way that I know you! And all those who believe in me also know that you have sent me! I have revealed to them who you are and I will continue to make you even more real to them, so that they may experience the same endless love that you have for me, for your love will now live in them, even as I live in them!"'

JOHN 17:20-26 TPT

When we are in Christ Jesus, accountable to others and aligned with a spiritual father or mother, we will burn for Jesus like we've never burned before. When a fire comes in contact with another fire, the fire increase even more. The fire of God will intensify and we will be ready to be released.

When To Be Released

The foundation should always be Jesus. When we have stepped into the appropriate structure, we will be sound to receive more. The more proportioned the structure, the easier it is to build upon. Jesus desires to set us on fire, but He wants the fire to last.

When we want the fire to last, we will become willing to die in the process. The fire of God not only establishes the nature of God but it also tests and purifies what's within us. (1 CORINTHIANS 3:10-17) The fire of God will test what's of God and then purify us from anything that's not God. We need the fire of God!

We can choose to either dismiss the fire or we can become carriers of fire. When we carry the fire of God, the warmth of Jesus will draw people near. Just as a bonfire draws people close so that they can absorb the warmth, so the presence of Jesus will pull in close those who recognize their need for Him.

We all can become carriers of fire for the glory of Christ Jesus! Everyone has the opportunity to burn for the Lord. Burning for Jesus is birthed out of a hunger for Jesus. We become hungry when we recognize our need for Him. It's not a formula and it's not a scientific problem, it's a relationship. True hunger is not birthed from frustration. In fact, frustration will choke out hunger. Frustration is an anxious cry out of a lack of security but hunger is a cry from fulfillment.

"Blessed are those who hunger and thirst for righteousness, for they shall be satisfied."

MATTHEW 5:6 ESV

"I have Jesus, but I need more of Jesus." This statement comes from wholehearted confidence that Jesus is who He says He is and that He will do what He says He will do. How do we stay hungry and desperate? How do we carry the fire of God into the world around us? We cannot carry the fire unless we are consumed by fire. Here are four ways that will help you be completely consumed by Jesus and keep the fire burning bright within you.

This is not meant to be a list nor an orderly routine. This is only meant to be a tool that helps establish a lifestyle that carries the fire of the God.

4 Ways To Carry The Fire Of God

Pursuing the Lord in surrender.

"Then Jesus said to His disciples, "If anyone wishes to follow Me [as My disciple], he must deny himself [set aside selfish interests], and take up his cross [expressing a willingness to endure whatever may come] and follow Me [believing in Me, conforming to My example in living and, if need be, suffering or perhaps dying because of faith in Me]."

MATTHEW 16:24 AMP

Carrying the fire of God begins with daily surrender. Surrender is key to establishing a thriving relationship with Jesus. In a relationship there is a willingness to sacrifice what we desire, for the one we love. This looks like us laying down our lives daily; giving up everything that is entangled in self promotion. Humility will sever the corrosiveness of pride in our lives. We must humble ourselves and hunger for His image. When we are willing to do whatever it takes to encounter Jesus, we will truly be hungering for His image and not our own. The heart of the Father wants to bring us back into our original design; being made in His image and walking in His presence.

Meditating on the Word.

"This Book of the Law shall not depart from your mouth, but you shall meditate on it day and night, so that you may be careful to do according to all that is written in it. For then you will make your way prosperous, and then you will have good success."

JOSHUA 1:8 ESV

Meditating on the Word of God is essential to carrying the fire of God. The word mediate means to think deeply. When I meditate on the Word, I not only read it but I have to make time to review it continuously. When we make time to meditate and review, we are giving value to what we are reading. The Word of God should have intrinsic value to us. Whatever is most valuable to us will be imbedded deep within us. (MATTHEW 6:21)

In meditating on the Word, we should also speak the Word. Resting on our tongue is the opportunity to release life or death. Every word carries power; the power to create or the power to destroy. Our words create our reality. (PROVERBS 18:21) All the more reason why it is imperative that our words align with the Word. When our words align with the Word, we will enter into Heaven's reality and our divine destiny.

Jesus is the Word and the Word made flesh. Allowing our lives to align with Jesus will open us to exploring facets of Jesus that we have yet to discover. To know Jesus, we must also know the Word. We have the opportunity to explore Scripture and expect an encounter with Jesus on every page. Our exploration, however, will only release transformation when we receive an encounter with Jesus. Whether a verse or even a word, something changes within us when we encounter the person Jesus. To carry the fire of God we must take the time to review the Word, speak the Word and ultimately encounter the Word. When the Word penetrates deep with us we will begin to shine forth the image and nature of Christ.

Loving from overflow.

"Jesus answered him, 'Love the Lord your God with every passion of your heart, with all the energy of your being, and with every thought that is within you.' This is the great and supreme commandment. And the second is like it in importance: 'You must love your friend in the same way you love yourself.'"

MATTHEW 22:37-39 TPT

Carrying the fire of God also means carrying the nature of God. The truest nature of God is love, because God is love. When His nature possess our being, we will overflow with Love. Love possesses us when we spend intimate time with the One who is Love. All of our thoughts, emotions and expressions, positioned in complete adoration. In this place of communion, we have the opportunity to be possessed by Love and out of the overflow of who He is, we have the ability to transfer Love to others. However, we can only transfer what we've received.

What have you received? The love of God compels us to love generously. His love isn't stumped by offense, but lavishly desires uncontained success for all. I've heard Dan Mohler use this analogy before on loving others in the same way we love ourselves:

When we are at the traffic light, everyone wants the light to turn for themselves. When the love of God possesses us, we'll actually desire the traffic light to turn for the other person first.

Offense has to bow it's knee to love that overflows.

Love transfers through a heart of faith. Faith is the confidence in things hoped for, and the conviction of things not yet seen. (HEBREWS 11:1) A heart of faith is seeing the goodness of God within each person even if it's not externally visible yet; seeing the way the Father sees. Hearts of faith create channels in which Love overflows to the other person. Love only overflows when we have a love that's on fire.

A love on fire is a love that is intimately interwoven in relationship. When a couple is madly in love, they introduce each other to everyone proudly and they will have an intense longing to be together. A love on fire is represented in the same way; we can't help but introduce people to Jesus and our greatest desire is to simply be consumed by Him.

Sometimes, however, a couple's love may grow cold. When this happens, the couple can be in the same room but feel distant from each other. If our love grows cold for Jesus, then we will slip into religion. When we slip into religion, our hearts will become hardened to relationship; feeling more distant from Jesus than ever before. Nowhere in Scripture does it say that the Lord walks away from us. In fact, Scripture declares the opposite, that God is for us and He is with us. It's time for us to invite the Lord back into the room of our hearts and ignite us with a love on fire again.

To carry the fire of God, we have to be intimate with the Lord; possessed by who He is, so that Christ's loving nature will generously overflow from our lives into the lives of those around us.

Extravagant generosity.

"Beloved ones, we must tell you about the grace God poured out upon the churches of Macedonia. For even during a season of severe difficulty and tremendous suffering, they became even more filled with joy. From the depths of their extreme poverty, super-abundant joy overflowed into an act of extravagant generosity. For I can verify that they spontaneously gave, not only according to their means but far beyond what they could afford. They actually begged us for the privilege of sharing in this ministry of giving to God's holy people who are living in poverty. They exceeded our expectations by first dedicating themselves fully to the Lord and then to us, according to God's pleasure."

2 CORINTHIANS 8:1-5 TPT

Extravagant generosity positions the atmosphere for breakthrough. The churches of Macedonia were a people who carried the fire of God! Despite their circumstances, they gave extravagantly. I would like to suggest that the churches in Macedonia gave extravagantly, not because of a principle, but because they were possessed by Love.

The people started with surrender; dedicated themselves first to the Lord. Then the churches looked beyond their own circumstances, and took the time to notice the Word; what God was saying and what God wanted to do. The churches of Macedonia then put forth the energy to move, in obedience, from the overflow of Love within them. Subsequently, resulting in the extravagant generosity of their resources; spontaneous giving and going beyond their natural giving limit.

The churches of Macedonia simply pursued the Lord in surrender. They knew His voice because they knew the Word and out of the nature of Christ that overflowed in their lives, they gave extravagantly.

The Lord is looking for those who will look past their own circumstances and sow into what the Lord is doing.

TESTIMONY

Several months back, a woman who had been living with our family for some time sowed financially into my wife and I. We never asked for money, but she said that the Holy Spirit impressed upon her to sow into us; to one she gave twenty dollars and to another she gave forty dollars. Unbeknownst to her, this amount helped take care of some of our families financial needs at the time. This woman began to explain that that sixty dollars was all she had to make it through the week. When she sowed the sixty dollars, the week had just begun. She continued to explain that she had to be obedient to the Holy Spirit's impressing even though she didn't understand why. The woman later told us privately that she was yelling and arguing with God, but yielded anyway. Later that day, this woman ran into a lady that she house sat for. This lady, whose house was watched while she was away, remembered that she forgot to pay this woman. So the lady reached into her purse and pulled out exactly sixty dollars. The woman who sowed into our family was amazed. On her way home, someone else stopped her and sowed into her financially because they felt impressed by the Holy Spirit to do so. The woman was overwhelmed with the love of God and we all were filled with such joy at what the Lord had done!

Carrying the fire of God goes beyond our wallets. People who carry the fire of God are ones whose lives are possessed by the One who is Love and Fire.

"Fire shall be kept burning on the altar continually; it shall not go out."
LEVITICUS 6:13 ESV

Jesus desires for us to carry the fire of God from nation to nation and never burn out! The question is, will we keep hungering for more of Him? There is more.

QUESTIONS

1. Why is it important to wait?

2. What are the two key guidelines that will significantly help keep the fire going?

3. What is the difference between accountability and alignment?

4. What are the four ways to carry the fire of God?

5. Who are the people that carry the fire of God?

CHAPTER SIX

There Is More

There is so much more to discover in our relationship with Jesus. True discovery will supercede our imagination and even our wildest dreams. Discovery begins with saying yes. We will experience the fullness of God to the point of overflow when we simply say yes to receiving more of God. The kingdom of God is positioned to add to and multiply what has been deposited into us; our assignments, our dreams and our resources. (MATTHEW 25:14-30) This Kingdom principle of stewardship and multiplication, furthers the Kingdom realm in the earth through the revealing of the friends of God and the sons of God.

Friendship

"For the greatest love of all is a love that sacrifices all. And this great love is demonstrated when a person sacrifices his life for his friends."

JOHN 15:13 TPT

True friendship with the Lord takes place when we engage within the truth of Jesus' love for us. Where Truth is settled within us and friendship is manifested from the relationship. Friendship is only built through a level of confidence and trust. Without these two components, it is our very nature to then shut down; creating no room for intimacy.

Friendships can be built off of "you scratch my back and I'll scratch yours." But true friendship lasts when we have nothing to gain from the other person. When we build friendships that are built on deep love without personal gain or agenda, we'll see relationships in our lives flourish. Every relationship begins with an act of love and an act of trust. Trust is built when there is something on the line for the relationship; when there is sacrifice. Jesus says the deepest love we can demonstrate is to lay down our lives for our friends. It's not that Jesus wasn't aware of his own needs, it's that Jesus placed his focus on the needs of others instead. We love because we are loved and we sacrifice because Jesus chose to sacrifice himself for us. Jesus is the greatest example of friendship. We have to realize that friendship is not just between us and others, but friendship should be engaged in our relationship with Jesus. Did you know that Jesus also said,

"You show that you are my intimate friends when you obey all that I command you."

JOHN 15:14 TPT

The reason I use the word "engaged" is because we get to play apart in accessing this specific aspect of the relationship. Just as we get to pick our friends and decide who we're close to, we have the opportunity to choose friendship with Jesus.

"You didn't choose me, but I've chosen and commissioned you to go into the world to bear fruit. And your fruit will last, because whatever you ask of my Father, for my sake, he will give it to you!"

JOHN 15:16 TPT

Friendship with Jesus is not a long distance relationship. We can sometimes project our busyness and failures on the relationship causing us to feel distant, less intimate and we can feel like Jesus has better things to do. True friendships are birthed when we become secure in the nature of the friend. When we are secure in the friendship, we will feel free to be ourselves; not pretending to gain attention. We have His attention, but does Jesus have our friendship? Friendship with Jesus is putting everything on the line and sacrificing our whole life to Jesus; whatever it takes.

Friendship with Jesus costs something. When we become friends with someone, we continue to grow to trust our friend, as well as learn to value their input. Our trust is then formed from a genuine love for one another. When we deeply love each other, we will value a friend's input. Jesus says, *"You are my friends if you do what I command you."* (JOHN 15:14) Our obedience will reveal our level of intimacy. Obedience is the gateway to closeness. When we choose to be obedient to His Word and the impressions of His Spirit, then we will access a deeper realm of intimacy with the Father.

There's this aspect within all of humanity that says "we get to decide what we want to do," it's called free will. Free will is the overriding mechanism within all humanity. Friendship with Jesus looks like sacrificing our ability to override the Father's heart. If we desire true friendship with Jesus, then we have to lay down our ability to say "no" to the Holy Spirit. True friendship with Jesus is birthed out of our deep love for him and out of our ability to yield to the Holy Spirit to say "yes."

Sonship

Sonship is birthed out of a kindred love. When my daughter was born, all I could do was hold her and tell her how much daddy loves her. Kindred love is locked with a great intimacy. Within the Father's heart, there is an overflow of intimate love. As sons, we have the opportunity to mirror back that same love.

Jesus submitted Himself to the will of the Father to die on the cross for our sins. True sonship manifests through submission, regardless of circumstances. Jesus said, *"not my will but yours be done."* (LUKE 22:42)

Submission within sonship is forsaking our desire for Him! We see a fascinating example of submission on the cross when Jesus said, "I thirst." (JOHN 19:28) We can easily relate this cry to a physical need and move on, but I believe there is something more to discover. From beginning to end, Jesus has been present in the presence of the Father; standing with the Father and revealing the nature of Father God. (JOHN 1:1) Jesus is in essence, righteousness and the standard of all righteousness. Without righteousness, we cannot obtain intimacy with the Father. (JOHN 14:6-7 & ROMANS 8:9-10) Jesus took on our sin upon the cross, but it was His death that positioned us to obtain righteousness. I'd like to suggest that Jesus' cry, "I thirst," was not out of physical desperation but out of a supernatural desire to see righteousness manifest within the life of all mankind so that all may experience the presence of the Father. Since the beginning, the Father's heart has been positioned for intimacy with His children. Scripture says,

"Blessed are those who hunger and thirst for righteousness, for they shall be satisfied."

MATTHEW 5:6 ESV

Jesus understood that sonship was about sharing in intimacy with the Father. The only thing that mattered to Jesus was what the Father said about Him. Jesus was more concerned with receiving His Father's smile rather than receiving the smile of others.

When we encounter the extremity and reality of the Father's love, through Jesus Christ, we will be positioned to believe for more.

Believing Is More

When we encounter the person of Jesus Christ, our faith will increase. The more can only be accessed in the presence of the Lord. Most everyone cries out for more but our human reasoning often quenches spiritual realities. The religious spirit often enables human reasoning to hinder God's love from forming inside of us. This causes many people to stop transforming into the image of Christ and conform to the ideology of the world. We become hollowed out shells that are filled by the world rather than holy temples where the Holy Spirit dwells. The Holy Spirit and His resurrection power in us is the revelation of the reality of Jesus Christ.

"Christ in you, the hope of glory" is not just for some day far off, it is for today. Jesus doesn't cease to live, He is still alive! Our faith should usher us into a place of living possessed by Love and walking in the presence of the Lord.

Living In Love & Walking In His Presence.

The following will help create a lifestyle where we live possessed by Love and walk in His presence daily.

Wait on the Lord.

"But they that wait upon the Lord shall renew their strength; they shall mount up with wings as eagles; they shall run, and not be weary; and they shall walk, and not faint."

ISAIAH 40:31 KJV

Waiting on the Lord is not waiting on Jesus to show up to a meeting. Jesus is already at the table. Jesus is simply waiting on us to turn our attention to Him. As our attention is turned toward the Lord, we have the opportunity to commune together; sharing our thoughts and feelings with each other. Jesus is worthy of our life and He is worthy of our time. In this place, our flesh often tries to distract us with the busyness of life and the daily to-do list. Jesus isn't looking for silence nor an abundance of words. Jesus is looking for a bride who will lock eyes with Him and whose heart is secure in His love.

Thanksgiving.

"Let us come into his presence with thanksgiving; let us make a joyful noise to him with songs of praise!"

PSALMS 95:2 ESV

We come into the Lord's presence, by faith, and we give thanks. When the veil was torn we were given the honor to come before the Lord ourselves! So let us come before Him with thanksgiving for the cross, His blood, His resurrection, His Spirit, His faithfulness and His goodness. Seeing the face of Jesus overwhelms our soul with His goodness. First and foremost, thanksgiving should be us ministering to the Lord. We have the honor to behold the majesty of the Lord. The Father is secure in His love for us, He doesn't need our praises; He delights in our praises. Through thanksgiving, we will enter into the Father's presence and we will bask in the Father's love. As we bask in the Father's love, our hearts will carry the privilege of honoring Him with our lives. We get to look to Jesus and adore him. Despite our circumstances, Jesus is worthy to be adored!

Worship.

"Through him then let us continually offer up a sacrifice of praise to God, that is, the fruit of lips that acknowledge his name."

HEBREWS 13:15 ESV

Through Jesus, we become living worshippers of the Father. Jesus even says, *"My Father is looking for those who will worship me in Spirit and in truth."* (JOHN 4:24) Worship is the sound of our lives confessing the name of Jesus. When we reveal Jesus by our lives, we are confessing Jesus as our Lord. We can only reveal the true nature of Jesus by the truth of His Word (JOHN 1:1-5) and by the power of the His Spirit (ACTS 1:8). Worship transcends what comes off of our lips, worship is poured out through our lives.

Enter into rest.

"Let us therefore strive to enter that rest, so that no one may fall by the same sort of disobedience."

HEBREWS 4:11 ESV

Entering into the rest of God is directly correlated with the Sabbath day of rest; when God rested on the seventh day of creation. (GENESIS 2:1-3) When God rested on the seventh day, Scripture doesn't say He took a nap. Often times, our culture limits the word rest, to mean naps. The rest of God isn't a nap, but doesn't exclude naps. Hallelujah! God has designed us for a day of rest. This rest God has designed us for has a greater value and importance than we often realize. When we don't rest, we become too tired to be obedient. The Holy Spirit may impress some things upon us such as people to love on, someone to share the Gospel with or even creative ideas. If we don't rest, we will slowly slip into disobedience; unable to fulfill the assignment He has set before us. Rest realigns us into a place of dwelling in the presence of the Lord. When we rest, we dwell. When we dwell, we walk in obedience.

Living a lifestyle that is possessed by Love begins with our attention completely fixed on His face. As our eyes are locked on the eyes of Jesus, His goodness will overwhelm our soul into a place of declaration and thanksgiving. Our worship will reveal Him and our rest will position us to dwell with Him. Our lives will be consumed by Jesus and no one will be able to escape His love.

Jesus desires that we would step into the deeper realms of our relationship with him. Will we become friends of God? Will we live as sons of God? Will we believe for more? More is only found in Jesus. When we allow our encounters with Jesus to actually change us into His image, the love of Jesus will percolate within our spirit man and permeate our sphere of influence. When we have a greater level of hunger, we will access greater realms of the love of God. Will you hunger for more of God?

QUESTIONS

1. Where does discovery begin?

2. How is friendship built?

3. How is trust built?

4. What has the Father's heart been positioned for since the beginning?

5. What are the ways we can live in the presence of the Lord?

CHAPTER SEVEN

Hunger For More

The only way we go deeper is by hungering for more. Hungering for more of God is not birthed out of frustration but out of the security we have in the relationship. When we become secure in the nature of Christ and who we are in Christ, we will no longer beg the Father like orphans but we will sit at the feet of our Father like children. We can't go deeper if we're still taking on the nature of an orphan. We must come to our Father and sit at His feet; listening and hungering for more.

Hungering for more not only takes us into the deeper dimensions of the relationship, but it also opens us to the realities of Heaven.

Living From Victory

Victory can only be obtained through Jesus Christ. Anytime we seek victory outside of Jesus we are utterly defeated. Jesus is the victorious one. There's no formula and there's no Plan B, it's only Jesus. When we try to access victory outside of Jesus, we choose to go to battle in our own strength. Battles can only be won through the anointing of the Holy Spirit.

We must war against spiritual forces, not earthly annoyances. Often times battles are being fought in the wrong way because we are waging war against a false, deceptive target.

About a year ago, my friends and I were ministering at a local high school. We had tents set up to feed students and then we built relationships with them. Our mission was simply to share the love of Jesus with the students. Many of the students were touched by the love of Jesus immediately but from the moment we got there was this one young man who shyly hung around the tent. Some of my friends tried talking with him but he was completely disengaged. This young man didn't have to hang around the tent, but he did. I felt the Holy Spirit impress upon me to go talk with him. So I walked up to the young man and began a conversation with him. This young man wouldn't look me in the eyes and kept looking away. I asked this young man where he was at with Jesus. He immediately told me that he knew who Jesus was but that he decided to go another way, to become a witch. We began talking about how Jesus is the ONLY way to Father God. After awhile, I told the young man to look at me, he did. I looked him in the eyes and told him that Jesus loves him. The young man said, "Okay." and quickly walked away.

Many times in life we will sow seeds of love in places where we may never personally see the harvest. Many might ask, "Can there still be victory even when we never see the outcome?" Victory is always found in love; who is Jesus. Just because we don't see an immediate transformation or manifestation does not mean there isn't victory. That day as we ministered at the high school, the love of Jesus was spoken and embedded in that young man's heart, and love always wins. We all can tell people that Jesus loves them. Jesus told us to love our neighbor, that includes every person around us. Jesus also gave us the example of a Samaritan man helping his "enemy" on the side of the road. Jesus warned the Pharisees to not just love those who loved them. Our hearts have to be open to love everyone and be secure in the Father's love even if they don't receive His love.

To step into the realm of victory we must have eyes to see and ears to hear what the Spirit of the Lord is saying and doing. Jesus would often tell a parable and say, *"This is why I speak to them in parables, because seeing they do not see, and hearing they do not hear, nor do they understand."* (MATTHEW 13:13 ESV)

In Revelation Jesus spoke to the churches and said the same thing. This is a call to awaken our spiritual eyes and ears to what the Spirit of the Lord is saying. When we see the Lord and hear what He is saying, we will have the opportunity to access new levels of obedience. It doesn't matter how good we look, there has to be fruit. Good fruit only comes from the Holy Spirit. Through the resurrection of Jesus Christ, the Spirit of God has imbedded victory into our lives. We begin living in victory when we receive Jesus and through the Holy Spirit, walk in resurrection power.

When we do this there will be an abundance of breakthrough.

Operating In Breakthrough

Breakthrough is the crushing of trials and the setting of our feet upon the rock. (PSALMS 40) I believe the biggest mistake we can make is when we hunger for

breakthrough more than we hunger for Jesus. The Lord always brings us out from where we've been. This would be impossible for us to do in our own strength. Total dependency on Jesus leaves no room for self sufficiency. We have to completely depend on Jesus and believe in Him for breakthrough. Too often we fixate on the problem rather than Jesus so we become weighed down by depression and paralyzed by fear.
Breakthrough doesn't mean to sit back. There are times where the Lord wants us to get up and break through. If we fixate our attention on the problem we will miss the solution. Breakthrough can only be found in the presence of Jesus; in His Spirit, in the Word, in our worship and thanksgiving.

"Let us come into his presence with thanksgiving; let us make a joyful noise to him with songs of praise!"

PSALMS 95:2 ESV

I'll never forget the Lord telling me that the culture of breakthrough is thanksgiving and praise. The Lord is surrounded in constant thanksgiving and praise. It's a part of Heaven's culture. Breakthrough is in the atmosphere of our praise and thanksgiving, especially in the midst of adversity and difficulty. The Lord's desire is to offer everyone freedom. His desire is for everyone to carry a light load. The only time my load gets heavy is when I stop praising and start complaining. Complaining shuts the door to breakthrough. In our greatest difficulty, shifting our focus from our problem to His face, changes everything; thanking the Lord for His faithfulness and praising the Lord for His goodness.

If we want breakthrough, we have to open up our mouth and praise from the vantage point of faith; trusting His nature over our situation. We praise from belief, not from what we see. Praising God and trusting His nature will continually transform us into a greater dimension of His glory. The greatest dimension of glory is the transfigured image of Jesus.

Hungering For More Of Jesus

If we want more of Jesus, we have to be willing to pay the price. Following Jesus wholeheartedly is not free. Jesus even said *"count the cost."* (LUKE 14:25-33) There are blessings but there are also persecutions. It's easy to highlight the good portions of Scripture, but we cannot preach a half truth. Following Jesus costs us our life. Jesus said,

"Whoever loves father or mother more than me is not worthy of me, and whoever loves son or daughter more than me is not worthy of me."

MATTHEW 10:37 ESV

Also Jesus says,

"And everyone who has left houses or brothers or sisters or father or mother or children or lands, for my name's sake, will receive a hundredfold and will inherit eternal life."

MATTHEW 19:29 ESV

TESTIMONY

About a year ago, I met a young man in a coffee shop. This young man was leading a ministry and was burned out. He began to desperately ask Jesus to show him if there was more. What this young man didn't know is that the Lord would give, not just him, but his entire ministry more. We began to meet regularly while also having bible studies with his group of college students. Many were overwhelmed with the love of God and were baptized in the Holy Spirit. As the weeks went on, the numbers grew and so did the salvations and baptisms. Suddenly, the attacks came. Some of the leadership of this ministry began to claim that this wasn't of God. These leaders then demanded all talk about the Holy Spirit to be shut down. As the situations escalated, I can remember this young man looked at me and said," I didn't know that following Jesus was going to cost me everything." This young man had a ministry and influence but also had a decision to make: was the God he had just encountered worth losing everything for?

Count the cost, because truly following Jesus means our lives will never be the same. Jesus desires for each of us to live from victory, operate in breakthrough and live in hunger for His image! If you truly want the image of Christ, then you have to decide, right here and right now, that your life will never be the same.

QUESTIONS

1. Where does the hunger for more come from?

2. Where is victory found?

3. What makes up the culture of breakthrough?

4. How do things shift in our greatest difficulty?

5. What does it cost to follow Jesus?

CHAPTER EIGHT

You Are Ready

The fire of God can now come and consume you. Are you ready to burn for the Jesus like never before?

"He will baptize you with the Holy Spirit and fire."
MATTHEW 3:11 ESV

Place your hand on your chest and pray this with me:

"Lord Jesus, I am open to you and willing to receive from you. Jesus, I ask that you come baptize me in your Holy Spirit and fire right now. I receive a fresh baptism of your Holy Spirit and fire! I receive all the gifts you have for me. I surrender my whole life to you again. I'm yours, Jesus! I'm yours, Jesus! I'm yours, Jesus! Thank you for filling me, Jesus. I ask that you would possess me with your love and let my life never be the same, in Jesus name. Amen."

You have now received THE promise of the Father. (ACTS 1:4-5) I am celebrating with you right now! Now you may be asking, "What's next?" In this chapter, we will identify what you now carry and the next steps to move forward in the Spirit.

What's Next?

You are now a generational witness of the resurrected Lord; Jesus Christ of Nazareth.

"But you will receive power when the Holy Spirit has come upon you, and you will be my witnesses in Jerusalem and in all Judea and Samaria, and to the end of the earth."

ACTS 1:8 ESV

What does it mean to be a witness of Jesus Christ? A witness for Jesus is one who preaches the full Gospel to reveal Jesus to the world. The following will help outline what the Full Gospel consist of.

The Full Gospel

1. Moved By Love.

"For God so loved the world, that he gave his only Son, that whoever believes in him should not perish but have eternal life. For God did not send his Son into the world to condemn the world, but in order that the world might be saved through him."

JOHN 3:16-17 ESV

We are first moved by Love to demonstrate the love of God. Love moves on the heart; softening hearts to receive Jesus Christ. His love, flowing through our lives, will make room to tell others about the sacrificial love of Jesus. You can begin with something as simple as, "Jesus loves you."

2. <u>Repentance.</u>

"And Peter said to them, "Repent and be baptized every one of you in the name of Jesus Christ for the forgiveness of your sins, and you will receive the gift of the Holy Spirit. For the promise is for you and for your children and for all who are far off, everyone whom the Lord our God calls to himself.""

ACTS 2:38-39 ESV

When people encounter the real Jesus, they'll experience His real love for them. Encountering Love, moves us into a place of repentance. Repentance isn't birthed from condemnation but rather God's goodness. (ROMANS 2:4) Condemnation doesn't change people, the goodness of God does. When we reveal Love, people will be overwhelmed by His goodness and drawn to repentance.

3. <u>Salvation.</u>

"because, if you confess with your mouth that Jesus is Lord and believe in your heart that God raised him from the dead, you will be saved."

ROMANS 10:9 ESV

Later Scripture says,

"But to all who did receive him, who believed in his name, he gave the right to become children of God, who were born, not of blood nor of the will of the flesh nor of the will of man, but of God."

JOHN 1:12-13 ESV

When the sons and daughters of God reveal the goodness of their Father, people will want to become children of God. Everyone wants a king like Jesus, who rules every heart with grace and truth. Jesus isn't ruling our hearts if He isn't ruling our lives. "Have you given your whole life to Jesus?" We all must confess Jesus as our Lord and believe God raised Him from the dead. Through this decision, we are instantly adopted into the family of God. This decision, giving our whole lives to Jesus, must go beyond a declaration and become an action.

4. <u>Baptism In Water.</u>

"Then Philip opened his mouth, and beginning with this Scripture he told him the good news about Jesus. And as they were going along the road they came to some water, and the eunuch said, "See, here is water! What prevents me from being baptized?""
ACTS 8:35-36 ESV

The baptism in water is an action which signifies dying to this life and being raised in new life. (ROMANS 6:1-4)

This is made possible through the death, burial and resurrection of Jesus Christ. Now each person has the opportunity to die to the flesh and live in the supernatural life.

5. Baptism In The Holy Spirit & Fire.

"I baptize you with water for repentance, but he who is coming after me is mightier than I, whose sandals I am not worthy to carry. He will baptize you with the Holy Spirit and fire."

MATTHEW 3:11 ESV

The baptism in the Holy Spirit and fire empowers us to manifest the image of Christ. The fire is more than an element, but it's a person; the person of Jesus Christ. The fire comes to establish, within us, an atmosphere of glory; the nature in which God always resides. There is no place in Heaven where there is no glory. Jesus moves Heaven and Heaven comes to live within us, not just to rest above us. The Holy Spirit comes to possess us while empowering us to manifest the image of Christ. We will manifest His image and witness well, when we move in power.

6. Move In Power.

"But you will receive power when the Holy Spirit has come upon you, and you will be my witnesses in Jerusalem and in all Judea and Samaria, and to the end of the earth."

ACTS 1:8 ESV

Power manifests the image and the reality of Jesus Christ. When we receive the baptism in the Holy Spirit and fire, we are given power to reveal how real Jesus really is. Power confirms the message of Christ and transforms lives. Without signs, wonders and miracles we cannot fully reveal Jesus to the world nor fully preach the Gospel. The focal point of power is the Son. Jesus has given us power to go!

7. Go!

"Go into all the world and proclaim the gospel to the whole creation. Whoever believes and is baptized will be saved, but whoever does not believe will be condemned. And these signs will accompany those who believe: in my name they will cast out demons; they will speak in new tongues; they will pick up serpents with their hands; and if they drink any deadly poison, it will not hurt them; they will lay their hands on the sick, and they will recover." So then the Lord Jesus, after he had spoken to them, was taken up into heaven and sat down at the right hand of God. And they went out and preached everywhere, while the Lord worked with them and confirmed the message by accompanying signs."

MARK 16:15-20 ESV

Going carries power because of the One who works with us. Going is established through our obedience not our performance. We will see more lives come to Jesus when our focus is on His image, not our own. The

Greatest Harvest can only be brought in through the full Gospel. The harvest will come forth as people are moved by Love, led to repentance, saved by Jesus, dead to this life, empowered to live in new life, manifest the image of Christ in power and obedient to go with the Lord.

"For I will not venture to speak of anything except what Christ has accomplished through me to bring the Gentiles to obedience—by word and deed, by the power of signs and wonders, by the power of the Spirit of God—so that from Jerusalem and all the way around to Illyricum I have fulfilled the ministry of the gospel of Christ;"

ROMANS 15:18-19 ESV

Generational Witness

Why are we generational witnesses? Simply because we desire nations and generations to know Jesus. If we steward our witness well, we will see atmospheres shift, along with generations altered and positioned to fulfill the call on their lives.

A great biblical example of a generational witnesses would be Paul's spiritual son, Timothy.

"I am reminded of your sincere faith, a faith that dwelt first in your grandmother Lois and your mother Eunice and now, I am sure, dwells in you as well. For this reason I remind you to fan into flame the gift of God, which is in you through the laying on of my hands, for

God gave us a spirit not of fear but of power and love and self-control."

2 TIMOTHY 1:5-7 ESV

Louis became a witness and her faith transferred and flowed down through many generations. If we want to see generations altered for the glory of God, we have to step into the full witness of Jesus; preaching the full Gospel and living possessed by the love of God. It's not enough to just be a church going Christian. People need to know Jesus! They need to know Love. The world is crying out for a people who will be possessed by Love and burn the nations with the knowledge of Jesus Christ. Will you?

"Jesus, release a bonfire in me!"

QUESTIONS

1. What does it mean to be a witness of Jesus?

2. What are the components of the full Gospel?

3. What is a generational witness?

4. Will you be possessed by Love and carry a bonfire to the nations?

ABOUT THE AUTHOR

Hunter Morris is a lover of Jesus and revivalist to the nations. From birth, Hunter was destined to awaken the nations with the knowledge of Jesus Christ. Since a young age, Hunter was on fire, preaching the Gospel and sharing the love of Jesus.

Hunter along with his beautiful wife, Jennifer and their precious daughter, Gracelyn reside in a suburb in Panama City Beach, Florida. Hunter currently travels around the world demonstrating the love of Jesus and loving people into the Kingdom of God. He has ministered in three continents and all throughout North America. Wherever Hunter goes, people are awakened to the love of God.

56110793R00054

Made in the USA
Columbia, SC
23 April 2019